The Heart of Esthetics

Creating Loyal Clients &
Achieving Financial Success

DIANE BUCCOLA

Copyright © 2013 Diane Buccola

All rights reserved.

ISBN: 1490992863
ISBN-13: 978-1490992860

DEDICATION

This book is dedicated to all of the hard-working estheticians who share my passion for the skin care business. Thank you for making the effort to continually educate yourselves so we can show the public that Estheticians Are a Girl's Best Friend!

And a special thanks to the members of SpaBizBoard who have been my biggest source of inspiration since 2006.

CONTENTS

1	A Note from Diane	1
2	I Love Esthetics	3
3	Client Development Plan	15
4	The First Impression	25
5	Menu of Services	33
6	Choosing (& Using) Your Space	43
7	Effective Marketing	47
8	Formula for Prosperity	65
9	Legal Issues	83
10	Networking	85

PREFACE

While the typical esthetician will take a multitude of classes to learn more about facial treatments and techniques, the same cannot be said for those who seek out vital information regarding how to build and maintain a successful esthetics business. So kudos to you for buying this book and taking the first step toward assessing your current situation with an open mind to possible changes.

For purposes of simplicity, I will occasionally use the term "Spa" to mean esthetic businesses, solo estheticians, day spas and resort spas (although I have included a few notes specifically for spa owners). While this book would benefit anybody in the spa business – or for that matter, any business that offers consumer services and products -- it is the esthetics business that will be prominently featured, as it has the potential to be the most profitable department in any spa-related business.

I will also use the word "she" or "women" when I am discussing clients, as typically the majority of our clients are women. However, I do not mean to exclude men. It is a wonderful thing that more and more males are flocking to spas and estheticians!

1. A NOTE FROM DIANE

As of this writing, I have been an esthetician for 18 years. I have worn a lot of hats in this business, as they say. But I have never been as excited and passionate about anything related to the spa business as I am about this book.

You know that feeling when you are watching a game show on television and the contestant is struggling to come up with the right answer; they have a lot of money on the line and the clock is ticking? You know the answer to the question so you are practically screaming at the television, as if somehow they will receive the vibe you are sending and they will blurt out the correct answer and win all of the money?! Well, that's how I feel when I hear estheticians struggle to find success in this business.

Because of my unique position as the owner of SpaBizBoard since 2006, I am aware on a 24/7 basis of the struggles of estheticians and spas. I know what the obstacles are and I know how to eliminate them. I know the wrong turns and I know the right turns. I know the paths that lead to struggle and I know the paths that lead to success. And I also know the bad advice that is regularly dispensed from consultants who are not actively involved in the esthetics business.

Our business is very different from all the rest. Ours is intimate and it is personal. And it is ever-evolving. So if an advisor is not currently hands-on in the treatment room, they are not necessarily the best-qualified to advise us.

I believe that we are only as strong as our weakest link, and I am on a mission to do everything I can to be sure the field of esthetics is strong and viable -- because your success is my success, and *our* success.

In this book, I talk a lot about passion. And esthetics is my passion. I am fascinated with the "psychology" of the esthetics business, such as what makes a consumer choose one spa or esthetician over another, or what compels a client to buy and others to walk away. There really is a science and a simple formula for success in the esthetics biz, and you are about to find out what it is!

2. I LOVE ESTHETICS

Things have certainly changed since esthetics first morphed from a "steam & cream" beauty treatment into a myriad of esthetic specialties. This book invites you to unlearn just about everything you have been taught or thought you knew about how to be successful in the esthetics business. You will be asked to dust off your dreams and remember why you were first drawn to the field of esthetics.

You may have wandered off of your initial path, quite possibly lured away by bad information or inaccurate training (or lack thereof), or maybe you are just drifting. Wherever you currently find yourself in the esthetics world, this book will offer clarity, specific solutions, proven strategies and the "magic" ingredient to success *(it's been there all along!)* which seems to be entirely overlooked these days.

So I suggest you keep a paper and pen, or notebook and highlighter nearby, so you can record your moments of inspiration and capture your ideas as they present themselves along the way. *Because they will.*

*The esthetics business rocks!
And we are so lucky to be a part of it.*

PASSION AND VISION

Spectators may think that it's the potential for profit and the ability to make a living that draws us to esthetics, and an action-packed menu of services that makes us successful. But those of us who are actually working in the treatment room know that in reality, it's *passion* that brings us here and *vision* that makes us successful.

*Logic will take you from point A to point B.
Imagination will take you everywhere.*
~Albert Einstein

Do you want to make a living, or create a life?
The ultimate success comes from living your dream and doing the work because it is a passion -- not just to earn enough money to survive. Passion for your work means that you would do it even if you were paid no money, because you just can't help yourself. Quite simply, *you love it*. Your work is a labor of love, and if you are one who believes in the Universal Law of Attraction[1] then you know that with passion comes inner fulfillment, outward success and bushels of money (if that is your goal).

---

[1] *Your dominant thoughts will find a way to manifest. You get what you put your energy and focus on, whether wanted or unwanted.*

Passion

The first step to success in the spa business is to carefully assess your current situation. To do that, I am going to ask you to try to remember why you were initially drawn to this business.

I have asked this question of estheticians many times over my years in this business and the answer is almost always the same, which is something along the lines of, *"I like to help people feel good."* Sound familiar? If that is your answer also, well, then, therein lies your *passion*.

Vision

It is very important that you do not allow other spas, esthetic businesses, or salons to affect your vision. Just because a spa or esthetician appears to be very busy, very well-known, or ever-expanding does not by any means indicate that it is profitable. And trust me, most business owners are not going to 'fess up to failures, so unless you have a look at their accounting records, you cannot possibly determine another's success.

It's true that the word "success" means many things to many people. Some simply want to have their name on the door and be a celebrity in their own town (or in their own mind). Others may just want a part-time gig that fits with their lifestyle. But this is about you, and only you can determine your definition of *success*.

So with an open mind and an open heart, dreams dusted off, and your imagination fired up and ready to go, ask yourself these questions and note the answers for future reference:

- What does *my* successful esthetics business look like in my mind?

- On a 1-10 scale (with 1 being *"not even in the ballpark, honey!"*), how close am I to my vision?

- What am I currently doing that *is* working toward my vision?

- What am I currently doing that is *not* working toward my vision?

- Are my current efforts taking me in the direction I want to go?

- What obstacles can I identify right now?

- Who around me is influencing me at this time?

- Is this a positive or negative influence?

Here are a few pearls of wisdom to take away from this chapter:

- If you changed only 1% a week, by year's end you would be 52% (more than halfway!) to your goal.

- Confirm your sources of info and advice. *(Ask questions!)*

- It's not how much money you make that counts, *it's how much money you get to keep!*

- Let the views of others educate and inform you, but don't model yourself after other spas and estheticians.

- A busy spa does not necessarily mean a successful spa.
- Don't be afraid to be different….*and better.*

I want to make this point very clear: *If your business is exactly where you want it to be, then you may not agree with some of the suggestions that I am offering.* And that's okay. But then again, if your business is exactly where you want it to be, you probably would not be reading this book.

What worked for us years ago may not be working now simply because times have changed and perhaps we are stuck. For those of us who are working hands-on in our treatment room, finding time to keep up with the ever-evolving world of esthetics may be difficult. So it is my goal with this book to offer a variety of suggestions in the hopes that you might find some ideas that are a good fit for you.

The best part about the esthetics business is that there are so many different paths to success. My wish is that something in this book helps you reach *your* ultimate success.

*Often in the winds of change…
a new direction is found.*

When I started my day spa in 2000, it was much easier to be successful. "Day spas" were a novelty, the idea being to bring the experience of a resort spa (which most people only enjoyed while on vacation) back home to their own neighborhood. Now, however, everybody is a "day spa" and the term has neutralized somewhat.

In my years in the spa business, I have seen day spas popping up everywhere. Every incarnation of doctor now has a "spa" of some kind, and hair salons call themselves "salon and spa." So the day spa does not have the impact, quality or meaning that it used to. Generally speaking, the term "spa" is an acronym for "**S**antas **P**er **A**qua" which translates to "healing with water," which as we all know doesn't necessarily apply to many of today's day spas whose only water source is the sink and a toilet.

So I propose that you carefully contemplate whether you really need to be a "day spa"? Consider every department in your spa and all of the services that you offer and determine which ones are profitable.[2] If you determine that being a day spa is no longer serving you well, maybe it's time for a change.

It is not necessary to be all things to all people, because typically you will be most successful with the services that you are passionate about and that you are really good at. Personally, I believe hair and nail services -- which are frequently noisy and may have unpleasant odors -- should not be contained within the same space as skin and massage services which are known for being quiet and tranquil with lovely aromas.

---

[2] *This will be discussed in further detail in Chapter 6, Choosing (& Using) Your Space.*

THE BAROMETER OF SUCCESS

Let's get this commonly-used excuse out of the way right now: "Tough economic times." *(If I had a nickel for every time I've heard that one...)*

I'm not disputing that times are tough, but that does not necessarily have to impact those of us in the esthetics business. For example, I refer you to the following statistic:

Top 10 Recession-Proof Jobs
"Not surprisingly, many of the 10 jobs involve health care or personal care. As Americans become more concerned about their health and appearance, occupations for those who can help them feel better are on the rise. Those include jobs for skin care specialists who work in spas and medical offices providing treatments that give patients a healthier appearance. **The field is expected to grow by 34 percent through 2016.**" *(Source: AOL.com 9/7/11)*

So now we know that the current economic situation is *not* the barometer for success. So then what is the barometer for success, you ask?

It is the **lives of women.**

Many customers who used to be able to afford pricey dermatology treatments are now looking for more cost-effective treatments, and that leads them directly to estheticians!

As things change -- including economically -- we must adjust. We must appreciate the trickle-down effect of changing economic times and plan for a change in our client base. It is a good time to consider becoming more clinically-trained and adding advanced treatments and/or abbreviated facials[3] to your menu.

Change is good for us and good for our clients. There is nothing worse than being boring....*and bored.*

> *Being "good enough" is no longer good enough.*

It used to be that having good products and an interesting menu was enough to lure clients to your esthetics business, and to keep them coming back. You didn't even need to be particularly skilled in the treatment room. However, as day spas gained in popularity, clients got more discriminating. And if you throw the changing economic times into the mix, you realize that we are literally competing with each and every business that sells absolutely *anything!*

CLIENT EXPECTATIONS ARE LOW

It is the sad truth that customer service has dropped to an all-time low. Consumers have gotten used to being ignored and mistreated when it comes to customer service. Below are a few common examples of generally poor customer service. Have you experienced any of these?

- ▸ You wait in line at a store to pay the cashier for an item you are purchasing. When the cashier hands your change back to you, what *should* happen is that you are sincerely thanked for having chosen to spend your hard-earned money in that store. But what typically happens is that it's

---

[3] *This is discussed in further detail in Chapter 5, Menu of Services.*

you who thanks the cashier -- *just for handing your change back to you!*

- Or one of my biggest pet peeves: You say, "Thank you" and they respond "No problem." (*NO PROBLEM?* It shouldn't be a problem to take my hard-earned money!) *"You're welcome"* is the appropriate response.

- When shopping at a clothing store, you head over to the fitting room to try on a few things. There is a limit to the number of items you can take into the dressing room. You hand over your extra items to a clerk, as is required; however when you are ready for your extra items, the clerk has disappeared -- causing you unnecessary inconvenience and stress.

- You go into a "seat yourself" casual restaurant only to find most of the available tables have not yet been cleared off, so there dirty tables and dishes are everywhere.

The good news about all of this is that if **you** provide really great customer service, it stands out. It is noteworthy. It will be a good experience for your customers and they will tell their friends. However, this is not simply a strategy to attract new customers. This has to be an ongoing effort among every department in your spa because given a choice, people will spend more money and more time in businesses where they feel that people care.[4]

---

[4] *Raving Fans, A Revolutionary Approach to Customer Service, by Kenneth Blanchard and Sheldon Bowles*

BASIC CLIENT NEEDS

Clients are pretty simple. They don't ask a lot of us, and we should be honored that that they come back time and time again for our services. But too many estheticians fall way short of meeting the client's basic needs, such as:

- A warm welcome and friendliness
- Respect
- Our full attention while they are in our space
- To feel valued and important
- To be sincerely thanked for their business
- To be invited to return
- To be remembered, even in their absence
- To be appreciated

How would you grade yourself in each of these subjects? If you are not yet an A+ student, the good news is that it is easy to improve. Put some thought into each of the above items and see if you can figure out where there might be room for improvement in your esthetics business.

For example, how do you greet your clients when they arrive? A handshake? A nod? Maybe a *"Hey, there!"* There is no right way, but we always need to be aware of how best to make each client feel really welcomed and comfortable when they are in our space.

Do you regularly check in with your client's level of comfort during a facial as to temperature of the room, the facial bed, the steam towels, or the hot wax? Are you good at sensing when it's time to stop the chit-chat during a treatment and encourage restful silence?

Do you take notes during each facial so that you can check in with the client at her next appointment regarding her likes, dislikes, and results from her last facial? Do you remember to ask how her products are working for her at home? Do you advise her when it's time to adjust something due to a change in weather or the current condition of her skin?

To be sincerely thanked feels so good to everyone. Unfortunately, it's not a common occurrence these days.

Remember, these people can be going anywhere for esthetic services, because as I pointed out earlier, there are spas on nearly every corner. Undoubtedly, there are cheaper places, snazzier spas, with prettier wallpaper, or whatever. But your clients choose you…..again and again.

That's a huge compliment and deserves a *"Thank you so much. It's always so good to see you and I'm looking forward to seeing you next month. Please let me know if you have any questions or need anything. Just give me a call and I'll get right back to you. Here's my card."*

There are so many ways to keep in touch with your clients throughout the year. The customary method is by way of a birthday card. Personally, I think that's fine, but it's just not all that special. Keep in mind that clients get those cards from many other companies, from car dealers to dry cleaners to airlines.

I suggest you do more unexpected things so that you stand out from the rest. After all, our relationship with our client is a personal one, and once a year we can afford to spend a little more time and money on our loyal clients. So while it's nice for them to know that you care just as much as their local pizza place, it would mean a lot more if you went just a little further to show your gratitude.

Take a moment and think about your annual profit on just one of your loyal monthly clients. Don't you think it's worth it to send one $25 floral arrangement once per year on her birthday? Or when she is coming in to see you any time near the date of her birthday, have a flower and a card lying on the facial bed when she arrives. Or maybe surprise her with a decadent piece of candy or birthday cookie.

Consider wrapping up a new product or gift item (something she hasn't purchased from you before) and give that to her as a birthday gift. It will be impactful and at your wholesale price, it's a bargain! An extra added bonus: You've just introduced her to a product she may want to purchase sometime in the future.

If you think about it, giving a facial is not all that tough. We all had to do it in order to graduate from esthetician school. But that is not really what distinguishes us from all the others. It's much more than that.

Every esthetician working today is providing facial services, but if you can master the art of *great* customer service, you hold the key to an enormously successful esthetics career.

3. CLIENT DEVELOPMENT PLAN

If you have been in this business for over a year and are still looking for new clients, *something is wrong.* Odds are that you – like most estheticians and spas – do not have a Client Development Plan (CDP) in place.

Getting people in the door is easy. Just put the word "FREE" on your front door and they will come. But creating long-term loyal clients is all about the relationship they have with *you*. Without a CDP, you are no different than a hamster on a wheel, going round and round and round. It might keep you busy, but success will always be out of reach.

The subchapters that follow will lay out for you the elements of an effective Client Development Plan.

NEW CLIENTS v. FORMER CLIENTS

Of course, if you are just starting out in the spa business, new clients are a necessity. However, for the rest of you, you should know one important fact: *It is TEN times more expensive to bring in one new client than it is to keep the clients you already have.* Yet probably the most common question that is asked of me by working estheticians is about how to attract more clients.

Rarely do business owners focus on how to keep their current clients loyal and happy, which also includes efforts to figure out why former clients have gone M.I.A. That's because spa owners and solo estheticians do not really understand that in our business, success is *not* built on selling treatments and products. Success in our business is built on **relationships**. So you can send unsolicited emails and hand out business cards all you want, but the end result won't likely be the esthetics career of your dreams.

Let's discuss the Client Relationship, because it is the Holy Grail of the esthetics business; it is the Fountain-of-Youth, the path to success, and it is the key that unlocks the door to esthetics nirvana.

We must wholeheartedly embrace the fact that our business differs from almost every other business out there. We are in an intimate business wherein we ask women to remove most of their clothing and get into what looks a lot like a bed. And even worse, we then remove their makeup and stare at them through a scary mag lamp. Could it be more distressing for the client?

So with that in mind, you can understand why our relationship with our clients should be our number 1 priority. It is at least as important (more, I think) as our skills in the treatment room and the products we sell.

A client will forgive you just about anything, if you have a solid bond.

THE CLIENT RELATIONSHIP

There are several components to the client bond and it's probably not what you think. Once you understand it, however, it's pretty easy to accomplish. At the very heart of it, it's just like a beautiful flower; if you don't properly tend to it, it will die.

The first time a client walks into your business, a potential relationship has begun. So even though she may have had a facial treatment elsewhere at some point in her life, it's imperative to make her comfortable from the very beginning of her relationship with you. This means that when she enters your treatment room for the first time, you should treat her as if she were a kindergartener walking into her very first classroom, and make a special effort to remove any obstacles or possible sources of discomfort for her.

For example, indicate not just with your words but also with a gesture so she understands exactly where her clothes, shoes, and accessories are to be placed once she has removed them. Be specific as to which items of clothing she must remove and which items are optional.

Hand the facial gown to her only after indicating how it should be worn; for example, hold it up to your own body and demonstrate how to fasten it. Next, pull the sheets back on the facial table so she understands she is to get *under* the sheets -- and be sure to mention *face up*. I know that sounds like a no-brainer, but you'd be surprised at the stories I have heard!

In other words, err on the side of "over-informing" your first-time clients. The last thing we want our clients to experience is any sort of discomfort. Causing a new client to feel inept or embarrassed can be a fatal flaw in the development of a fledgling client relationship.

The Intake Form

Handing the client a pen and asking her to fill out your intake form is a mistake, as this important step is so much more than information on a page. This is a huge opportunity to bond with the client as you ask the questions, record the answers, answer questions she may have, and discuss various items and issues during the process. This is a personal experience for the client who is oftentimes providing private information, and it should be treated respectfully and with great care.[5]

Display your CE Certificates

Use the walls of your treatment room to further the bond with your clients and gain their trust. There is nothing more comforting for a client who might be feeling a little intimidated as she reclines in the facial chair, than glancing around your treatment room and seeing evidence of your vast knowledge and experience.

My suggestion is that you frame your Continuing Education certificates and hang them on your treatment room wall. That has a much better impact than any poster or piece of art. Make the display as artsy or clinical as you wish, to reflect your personality and work environment. Just don't waste that precious wall space!

Listen to their Story

You've got a semi-naked woman without makeup in your facial chair or table. Let her tell you about her current skin condition, product usage, facial history, etc. Of course, you can figure this

---

[5] *The intake process will be discussed in more detail in Chapter 8, Formula for Prosperity.*

out yourself, but it's her story. Let her talk; you listen. If you create a strong bond in the beginning, you will have a loyal client for years and you can talk as much as you want to. This conversation will happen effortlessly during the intake process as you go through the intake form with her.

One Good Thing

Of course, your job is to identify and resolve any issues with her skin and her home care habits. But somewhere in all of that, the client can feel burdened with the diagnosis. So try to find at least one thing that is *right*, something that is good about her skin or her skin care regimen. It will be a gift that she needs and will not soon forget.

Notes and Records

Recording which services you provided as well as noting the products you used during each appointment is vital to the client bond. You will then be able to refer back to your notes so you can inquire about the results of her previous facial and any reactions she may have had to the treatment. Additionally, you can refresh your memory as to any particular condition she may have been struggling with at her last appointment so you can determine whether there has been any improvement. Based upon that information, you can then calculate what your next treatment should be.

You should also note any upcoming travel plans she may have so you will recognize the possible cause of any dehydration or hyperpigmentation that might result. And don't hesitate to record personal details about her children or her work so you can inquire about that next time. This shows an expression of interest in your client and will go a long way to further the client bond.

Know your Products

A client will be comforted by your passion and knowledge of the products you are using on her. Most clients don't care so much about ingredients and names of products. What they want to know is: "What will it do for me?" Therefore, product knowledge training for estheticians is imperative.

This is a common mistake made by spa owners and managers. They don't realize that it is extremely beneficial for their bottom line to send their estheticians for product training on every product they are expected to use and sell. This education is a make-or-break investment in the success of the spa.

✌ NOTE to SPA OWNERS:

A common fear is that if you provide your estheticians with training, someday they may leave your spa and take your clients with them. While that is a legitimate concern, it is not an insurmountable one. Spa owners and managers must also make an effort to create a solid bond between the client and the spa. This will insure that the client will choose to stay with the spa even if her regular esthetician is no longer there.

The best way for a spa to create that loyal bond is simply to show their clients that they care. This starts with stellar customer service offered by the owner, manager, front desk and all other employees that clients encounter before and after they step into the treatment room. A warm hello goes a long way.

Other important factors are the location of the spa, easy parking, convenient hours of operation and personal service whenever possible, instead of all communication via online booking and social media. Very often, the spa can afford to offer additional perks that another spa or solo esthetician cannot afford. So keep that in mind and use it to your advantage. ✌

Discounts

Personally, I am not a fan of discounts. Statistically speaking, you will only attract people who are looking for a deal, and when the discount is gone so will be those clients. So I suggest leaving discounts to those in the business of food service and car washes, etc.

One of the biggest mistakes that estheticians and spas make -- and I see this all the time – is the *"10% off on your first facial"* marketing strategy. First of all, it is so overdone that it has little or no impact. But much more importantly, it is so insulting to your existing clients! They come to you month after month, year after year, and they have to pay full price while somebody new *(who may never return)* gets a discount? If that is part of your current marketing strategy, you may want to rethink that one.[6]

Freebies

Freebies, on the other hand, can work well as long as you use this strategy wisely. By this I mean giving away something that costs you very little, such as a sample product or an a la carte service. Some suggestions are:

1. A free brow or lip wax or sugar with a specific facial treatment (can be limited to specific period of time). This is a good way to introduce your facial clients to your hair removal services and create new waxing or sugaring clients.

2. Giving away a sample of a product to existing clients. Be sure to give a sample of something *they are not already using* so that you are introducing them to something new, which ultimately they will want to purchase in the future.

---

[6] *A better option for first-time clients is discussed in Chapter 5, Menu of Services.*

3. Free Introductory Consultation and Skin Evaluation. This is such a great way to get potential clients into your business. But of course, it is what you do once they are in the door that will determine if they ultimately become a regular, loyal client.[7]

BE THE CLIENT

The Skin Care Magnet

If you want to quickly, easily and inexpensively mesmerize a potential new client and have her immediately submit to your wisdom and expertise, just put her in a Skin Scanner! [8]

For those of you who are not familiar with this piece of very basic equipment, it is simply a Wood's Lamp that is encased in a plastic box with a window on the outside and a mirror on the inside. The esthetician peers through the window while the client views her UV'd reflection in the mirror.

There are other methods such as the high resolution, hand-held microscope that hooks up to your PC, tablet or Smartphone. With this system, you place the hand-held tool on the client's skin and the magnified image appears on the screen. A version of this system also allows for capturing and saving digital photographs that you can keep in your client's computerized file for future reference so you can track improvement.

These are very powerful esthetic tools. The esthetician has an opportunity to explain the various conditions that are visible such

---

[7] *More about the intake process in Chapter 8, Formula for Prosperity.*

[8] *Also known by various other names such as Skin Scope.*

as sun damaged areas, skin in need of exfoliation, oily areas, etc. This is a wonderful opportunity for the Esthetician to suggest and explain various treatments and home care products.

Those of you who are already using any of these scanning devices know that the images can be eye-opening and enlightening to a potential new client, and from that point, they will do whatever you tell them to do!

Assess your Treatment Room or Spa

This sounds like a no-brainer but trust me, as important as it may be, it is rarely considered. You *must* periodically remove your esthetician hat and become the client for 15 minutes. See things as a client would see them. Here is a checklist:

1. Lie on your facial table. Is it comfortable? Look upwards. What does the client see? Stained ceiling tiles? Dirty fan blades? Look around at the art on the walls and accessories. Are they dusty? How about the sheets and towels, are they worn and dingy? Check the wax pot. Is it gross? What about cleaning supplies, and other storage items? Is everything out of sight as much as possible?

2. Size up the state of any common area that may be used by a client; for example, the bathroom. What do they see? (Hopefully you've got the feminine hygiene items stored out of sight, at least.) What about hair brushes, bathroom supplies, etc. If you don't have cupboard space, then buy some inexpensive baskets or decorative boxes and stack them.

3. Is your retail area clean? Are the shelves and products dusty? Is your signage legible?

4. Your front desk should be a thing of beauty. That simply means uncluttered and easy for the client's use such as for product purchase, payment and scheduling of appointments.

5. Study your employees. Are they clean? Dressed properly? Do they smell okay? What about fingernails and toenails? Should you consider instituting a "no sandals" rule at work?

6. And lastly, don't forget to mystery-shop your front desk staff. Have somebody whose voice won't be recognized call in to make an appointment or ask questions. Listen in. It's important that you know if there is something that needs improvement because the first contact a potential client has with your spa is a *make-or-break* moment for your business.

℘ NOTE to SPA OWNERS:

Very often women will go to the spa with a friend, and afterward they are very likely to compare their experiences. This is why it is crucial that your estheticians are trained to follow similar protocols for each of the facials on your menu. Of course, the esthetician's personality and style will define each facial, but the basic elements should be the same. ℘

4. THE FIRST IMPRESSION

The first contact potential clients may have with your spa these days might be via social media. Social media has changed the communication landscape, that's for sure. Gone are the days when clients and potential clients received personal service on the phone when scheduling their appointments. This was the spa's chance to make a great first impression and set themselves apart from the others. It was also an opportunity to up-sell their services before an appointment was made.

Also gone by the wayside are personal phone calls to remind clients of their upcoming appointments. Now it's online appointment scheduling and reminders by email or text. Yes, it is extremely convenient for us, but it does not give businesses the right to neglect personal interactions in their social strategy – especially in the esthetics business. When it comes to success in the spa business, at the end of the day, people still buy **from people.**

Has social media lost its power of persuasion?

It seems like only yesterday that social media marketing was a new and exciting opportunity. (And it really was!) But times have changed and now social media is commonplace. So you better know how to get the most out of it.

Before embarking on a social media campaign, it's important to have a clearly-defined goal and identify an intended outcome. Have you done a detailed audience analysis? For example, do you want people to sign up for your mailing list? Do you want to sell them a particular product or service?

Ask yourself why you are online and then use the answer to determine your goals and specifically how social media can help you meet those goals. Otherwise, social media marketing is as ineffective as casting a wide net over a large area and hoping to catch something/anything.

Duplicating what everybody else is doing is the fastest way to mediocrity, and there is no way to stand out when you are mediocre. You blend in with everyone else; you are unremarkable and forgettable. By limiting yourself only to social media marketing, you run the risk of ignoring potential clients such as perhaps anti-aging clients -- and more specifically, the Baby Boomer generation -- some of which may be using social media, but not necessarily to research products and services.

Consumers are hit with a constant barrage of information from television, social media, emails, etc. These days your email address is required for *everything*, and your personal info ends up in a multitude of databases used for marketing purposes and surveys.

I often hear spa consultants advise estheticians and spa owners to "capture" people's email addresses for marketing purposes. The problem is that as a society, we are drowning in emails, and this type of covert marketing just doesn't work anymore. I'm not suggesting these sorts of marketing strategies won't work for somebody, but our business is very different.

E-newsletters are often not being read and/or are being unsubscribed from; and even if they are being opened, they are not eliciting a response from clients or potential clients. Emails are being ignored or deleted because not only is it impossible to stand out in somebody's email box with limited visible info such as only the sender's name and subject line, but email marketing has become an annoyance.

Even more annoying, I think, is the fledgling practice of sending unsolicited text messages to promote goods and services. Not only is this an interruption to a client's day, but depending on a person's text message plan, they could be charged for those texts. And in our business, a source of annoyance is definitely *not* what we want to be.

Cheaper and faster does not necessarily mean more effective. So use your social media strategies as one tool in your marketing kit, but not at the expense of abandoning personal contact with clients and potential clients.

And don't dismiss a useful "snail mail" marketing campaign. Snail mail is experiencing a resurgence because while it's easy to completely ignore an email, and be irritated by an unsolicited text message, with snail mail they will at least have your info in their hand at some point -- even if it's only long enough to place it into the recycle bin.[9]

You want to be sure your envelope is noteworthy. Add a seasonal sticker, use a colored envelope or colored pen. Hand-address it, so it looks more personal. Spray it with perfume? *(Just kidding!!)*

Research shows that there are a couple of sure-fire elements in a print or mail campaign that will attract attention, which is the first step in getting your message across:

- **A photo of a person.** People will always glance at something that contains a photo, simply to see who is in the photo and to determine if perhaps they might know the person(s) in the picture.

- **Put the most important piece of info at the top.** People are barraged with information all day long and it can turn into mindless clutter in their brains. Your first piece of information should carry enough weight to entice them to keep reading down the page.

    If you waste that important area by starting with your company name or logo or some cutesy introduction, you've lost them. They will not bother to read further and therefore will miss your message entirely. However, if you capture their attention at the top, they will eventually seek out your company info at the bottom of the page.

- **Make it easy to read.** Choose an easy-on-the-eyes color and print, such as a dark-colored text on a light-colored

---

[9] *More about newsletters in Chapter 7, Effective Marketing.*

background. Don't make clients and potential clients have to work hard to read your message, or they won't. For example, if they have to get up to get their reading glasses, they'll likely skip it…and you.

Business owners need to know where to draw the line on social media marketing.

SOCIAL MEDIA TRENDS

Facebook
Very common these days is a focus on Facebook marketing. Everywhere, we see *"Like us on Facebook!" "Find us on Facebook!" "Visit our Facebook page!"* which while that may result in a lot of "Likes," it doesn't necessarily capture any Fans or Friends who will ever actually purchase anything.

Do you realize that Facebook – *not **your** business* -- is reaping the benefits of your Facebook promotions?! Of course, we all should have a presence on Facebook, but endlessly promoting your Facebook page only drives clients and prospective clients **to** *Facebook…* instead of to your website!

Groupon
Groupon is one of many collective buying sites that have burst on the scene and can be hard for most small businesses to resist. By offering deep discounts, these sites offer the potential to attract big numbers of clients and sales. But is it a good idea for *your* business? Groupon built its business working for consumers -- not small businesses.

The most important element to consider when deciding whether to jump on the Groupon bandwagon is whether or not that marketing strategy has the potential to develop long-term repeat clients, which we all know is the real "bread and butter" in our business.

Consider whether the typical Groupon user is a good fit for your business: This individual's main goal is to find a good deal because he or she does not want to pay full price. Therefore, these people are very unlikely to become repeat clients unless you continue to offer the same deep discounts.

Also consider the effect on your current long-term clients. In spite of their continued loyalty to you, they are required to pay full price for your services while the Groupon clients get the discounted services. This definitely falls into the "bad customer service" category.

Basically, Groupon is just an advertisement disguised as a coupon with a temporary shelf life. And once the coupon no longer exists, the consumer's interest disappears as well.

Online Scheduling

Online appointment scheduling is growing in popularity as people become more comfortable and proficient with the internet. The advantages are many for both the client and the business: The client has the ability to schedule an appointment 24/7 without having to call in and be put on hold by a busy front desk staff -- or worse, having to wait for a return call. Another benefit is that the business can check the work schedule from anywhere at any time, and many happy users claim that no-shows are greatly reduced. That's the good news!

The not-so-good news is that an important personal connection between a client (or a potential client) is lost when we no longer communicate with them directly.

We are in an intimate business in which success is measured by our personal connection with people.

With 100% online scheduling, lost is the very important first conversation with a potential new client who would greatly benefit from talking to someone that could help her navigate the spa menu or answer her tentative questions. Those are important *moments of truth* that can make or break an esthetics business or spa.

Reach your Demographic
Of course, if you offer hair removal services in a college town, you can bet that social media is reaching your customers. However, if you are interested in the anti-aging business, don't make the mistake of overlooking the lucrative Baby Boomer generation. Yes, they are on social media, but they may not be as active as those who grew up with social media.

A Website is Mandatory
Even if you are not particularly internet savvy, you really must have a website. People of all ages and income levels are seeking out information online, so you need an online presence. There are many user-friendly and inexpensive build-your-own websites that you can create and manage yourself if you do not care to invest in a highly-technical website.

All that is really required is basic information, such as your contact info, hours of operation, menu, and some information about who you are. The most important information – such as what makes you and your services special -- needs to be on your landing page (the first page they see when they arrive at your website). If they like what they see there, they will continue to explore your site and will look for your contact info.

In Summary
While it is easy to follow the crowd into the land of social media, that is not necessarily the best path to success in the spa business. Rather, we must very carefully consider the totality of our marketing strategies. Social media of course has its place, but in our business specifically, we must not forget the need for personal contact outside of the treatment room.

5. MENU OF SERVICES

When a consumer considers a spa menu, he or she almost always has only one question in mind: *"What's in it for me?"* In other words, they want to know what benefits they will get from the facial. But very often, spa menus are too complicated for the average consumer (and by "average consumer," I mean anyone who is not a trained esthetician) nor does it answer that all-important question: *What's in it for me?*

Deciphering our Code
Read the Pomegranate Peel and Blueberry Peel descriptions below which I have cut and pasted from a prestigious spa's menu. I left in the typos from the Blueberry Peel description (which are noted in *italics)* to emphasize how important it is that we proofread our menus or ask somebody to do it for us if perfect spelling and grammar are not among our many talents.

Of course, flawless spelling is not a requirement to be a great esthetician. Some of the most brilliant and talented people can't spell very well. However, misspellings in a menu indicates that the esthetician (or spa) is careless, and that can be enough to keep some potential clients away. It is such an easy thing to fix, so there really is no excuse not to have a properly-written menu of services representing you.

- **POMEGRANATE PEEL**: Lavish your skin with antioxidants to prevent free radical damage and support the life span of healthy cells. This peel works beautifully to soften and exfoliate your skin, while adding anti-inflammatory and antioxidant protection.

- **BLUEBERRY PEEL**: Suitable for all skin types, this refreshing peel exfoliates with Lactic Acid and Vitamin C, then purifies the *skn* with the powerful antioxidant properties of blueberries. The hydrating benefits of D-Glucuronic Acid are the finishing touch to this *wonderfull* gentle, yet effective peel. Although new, this is already one of our most popular treatments to exfoliate, purify, and smooth the skin.

Let's break down the elements of the Pomegranate Peel and assess it from a client's perspective. And later you can dissect the Blueberry Peel as if you were the client. (Probably starting with *"Will blueberries make my skin turn blue?"*)

Pomegranate Peel:
Lavish your skin with **antioxidants** to prevent **free radical damage** and support the life span of healthy cells. This peel works beautifully to **soften** and **exfoliate** your skin, while adding **anti-inflammatory** and antioxidant protection.

1. **Antioxidants** – *A client may know the definition of "antioxidants," but it is doubtful that the average client understands specifically how antioxidants are related to skin damage and skin care.*

2. **Free radical damage** – *same as above. It's a complicated process that the general public may not understand; i.e., the connection to skin care.*

3. **Soften** – *The descriptive words usually associated with skin care are more along the lines of "tighten" and "firm;" in other words, the opposite of "soften"!*

4. **Exfoliate** – *This is one of the most important words in the esthetic dictionary, however, it is unfamiliar to many consumers.*

5. **Anti-inflammatory** – *Everyone knows that inflammation is not a good thing, but not everybody understands how it relates to skin damage and skin care.*

Our Code Deciphered

Here is an example of a more user-friendly description of a facial treatment. Keep in mind the potential client's question, *"What's in it for me?"*

> ### *Hydrating Facial:*
> There's **dry**, and then there's <u>really</u> DRY. The **easy solution** is the **soothing, super-hydrating** effects of collagen. The **frequent flyer's** best friend, and definitely the facial you want **before a party or photos**. You **glow**, girl! *Recommended for Baby Boomers, mature, menopausal and dry skin types.*

Now let's dissect the Hydrating Facial:

1. **Dry** – *Everybody knows this word, and it is a very common skin condition that estheticians are regularly asked to resolve.*

2. **Easy solution** – *This is self-explanatory, of course. Both of these words are optimistic and comforting to clients.*

3. **Soothing** – *Easily recognizable to clients, optimistic, comforting.*

4. **Super-hydrating** – *The obvious solution to the common dry skin complaint.*

5. **Frequent flyer, before a party or photos** – *Makes it clear who specifically might benefit from this facial.*

6. **Glow** – *Who doesn't want to glow after a facial?!*

7. **Recommended for Baby Boomers, mature, menopausal and dry skin types** – *It's abundantly clear who will benefit from this facial.*

UNCOMPLICATE YOUR MENU

First-Timer Facial

During my Business Essentials 101 class, I ask the attendees a specific question, and 99% of the time somebody in the class gets it right. Here is that question:

When a potential first-time client calls a spa, what question do they always ask?

And the correct answer is: *"How much are your facials?"*

These potential clients do not ask this question because they really want to know the price. They ask it because they don't know what else to say to whomever answers the phone. And what is the typical response from the front desk staff? They give the price of the spa's lowest-priced facial, of course. *And that's a problem!*

Properly-trained reception staff knows that this is the most often asked question by callers, and they are prepared to engage in conversation with those potential clients.

To make this situation easy on my reception staff as well as any potential client who calls in, I created what I call the "First-Timer Facial" (FTF). It's not a fancy name, but it serves the important purpose of making it *really* clear for whom this facial is intended.

The FTF has a set price and a specific amount of time, but the components of the facial are determined when the client arrives and meets with the esthetician. What this means to the client is that he or she does not have to know his or her skin type or current skin care needs, and is not forced to choose a facial from a complicated spa menu. After all, it's not the responsibility of the client to determine which facial service she needs. That is the most important component of a professional esthetician's job.

The FTF eliminates the need for the front desk staff to "sell" any particular facial. Whomever receives the potential client's phone call only needs to know the components of the FTF and be able to explain to the caller that his or her facial will be determined in conjunction with the esthetician after a detailed consultation and evaluation.

So with the FTF, the pressure is taken off the client **and** the front desk, so trust in the esthetician's expertise and the bonding process has already begun.

- ▸ FTF must include 15 minutes of pre-facial consultation/chat time as well as 15 minutes post-facial for discussion and recommendation of home care products and regimen.

Customized Facials

We need to keep up with the times and be in touch with the needs of our demographic. Therefore, a lengthy facial menu may not be serving you well. As clients veer away from pricey treatments offered by dermatologists, they are looking to estheticians to provide clinical facial services. This doesn't mean you can't also have a relaxing facial or two, but you should incorporate into your menu facial treatments that are customized specifically to your clients' needs.

While the elements of the customized facial may be the same (cleanse, exfoliate, mask, etc.), the products chosen will be customized for each client's current skin care needs. I am a firm believer in having two levels of facials[10] which for purposes of this chapter, we will call:

1. Bells & Whistles facial (B&W)
2. Basic facial (Basic)

The B&W will include everything but the kitchen sink, to use an old familiar phrase. It will include use of various esthetic equipment, extractions, deep exfoliation, eye treatment, hand treatment, upgraded mask, massage, and whatever else you want to add. And it will cost at least $20 more than the Basic facial. On the other hand, Basic will be the shorter, simpler, typical facial.

My suggestion is that you *always* treat a first-time client to the B&W, but charge them the price of the less expensive Basic facial.

---

[10] *This does not include specialty treatments such as peels, clinical acne treatments, etc.*

The reason is that after experiencing the B&W, it is highly unlikely that the client will ever want to downgrade to the Basic -- even though it means they will have to pay full price for the B&W in the future. This works every time, and it completely eliminates the challenge of up-selling.

Abbreviated Facials

As was mentioned in an earlier chapter, the barometer for success is the lives of women. This means we must be ever-mindful of women's esthetic needs *and personal needs* and be willing to change with the times.

One such change is that many women don't have the time in their day (or week or month) for a lengthy facial. And it's not only the time involved for the facial itself, but also what I call "post-facial recovery" time, which refers to the fact that some women are uncomfortable going out in public directly from the facial room.

This means they either have to go home and stay there, or go home and fix themselves up before resuming their day. So this is an obstacle that we need to remove to make it easier for female clients and potential clients. If you don't have a facial designed to accommodate the lives of busy women, you are missing out on a lucrative source of revenue.

I suggest adding a facial treatment that does not require changing into a facial wrap and avoids the resulting "post-facial hair" that comes with having her head tightly bound in a head wrap. Instead, lightly drape a bath towel across her chest (over her clothes) and a hand towel around her hair, gently tucking it below her ears so that when it's removed, her hair in still intact.

This condensed facial would be streamlined so that it is less time-consuming, and products chosen for the treatment would be mindful of her need to go on with her day once she leaves you. An example would be a lift-off mask that does not require removal with water.

If you also offer makeup services, a sure-fire up-sell would be a 10-minute daytime makeup application. With that service also comes the possibility of makeup sales, so it is a win-win.

I don't recommend calling this abbreviated facial a "Mini Facial" as that is overused and stale. Additionally, the term "Mini Facial" indicates that it is not a full facial. And in truth, just because a client doesn't have to change into a facial wrap and the mask is quicker does not mean that it's not a full facial.

So make it a **real** facial. Name it something fun like "Glow-on-the-Go!" Or use skin-specific serums and name it "Targeted Facial Infusion." Whatever you call it, be sure the benefits of the facial are made clear to clients and potential clients. Remember to always keep in mind the client's all-important question: *What's in it for me?*

Maintenance (VIP) prices

One really great way to insure prompt rebookings and prevention of no-shows is to offer two-tiered pricing. What this means is that if a client rebooks or schedules a series of appointments in advance, they will pay a slightly lower rate. For example, if your regular brow wax price is $25, the "maintenance" price would be $20.

To qualify for the maintenance pricing, the client would have to schedule her next appointment *as she is leaving her current appointment*[11] and her next appointment would have to fall within the window you require, say 3-4 weeks. However, if the client books the appointment but does not keep the appointment, the regular $25 pricing would then apply.

This can also work with facials. Maintenance pricing would be $10 or $20 less, depending upon the regular price of your facials.

Another name for this two-tiered pricing could be "VIP" pricing. Applied this way, clients who take advantage of the two-tiered pricing would think of themselves as VIPs, and who doesn't want that?

---

[11] *You may choose to extend this offer to a client who does not book her next appointment as she is leaving because perhaps she needs to check her calendar; as long as when she does book her next appointment, it falls within the required timeframe.*

6. CHOOSING (AND USING) YOUR SPACE

It is very important that you give some careful thought to exactly what sort of clientele you wish to develop. For example, will you rely on walk-in traffic? If so, you've got to be located where people will not only be able to see your building, but also be able to read your sign as they drive or walk by.

While being located on a busy street might be a good thing, if prospective clients are whizzing by in their cars, will they even notice you? And if your name is generic ("What's-Her-Name's Day Spa"), will they comprehend what sorts of treatments you offer or what services you specialize in? Think about how you would market yourself in this location.

My day spa was located on a busy street and I used an old-fashioned sandwich board sign at the curb to get drivers' attention. It worked really well for me, but before opting for this signage, it's important to note the speed limit on the street, the direction of travel and which way drivers will likely be looking as they pass by. Also, be sure to check your city or county's regulation regarding sandwich board signs, as sometimes they are prohibited.

My sign was very simple, because there was not a lot of time to grab the drivers' attention as they sped by. So my sandwich board sign said simply: "Facials" "Massage" "Waxing," at the top, followed by my company name and phone number.

Of course, I knew that drivers wouldn't see all of that information in the few seconds they had to glance at my sign. But I knew if they at least saw "Facial," "Massage," and "Waxing," they would know what services I offered, which is the most important thing. And they probably could remember at least the first word of my business name (which was "SKIN"), so they could look me up later. And if they really wanted to know, they could circle back and get the phone number from the sign, or maybe even stop in.

That marketing technique was very inexpensive yet extremely successful for me. But if I would have put too much information on that sign, or if the writing was too small, it would have been a flop.

If you prefer to attract a younger crowd, put yourself near their schools or colleges, or at least on the path to wherever they might be going. If the 30s and 40s age group is attractive to you, find an elementary school, shopping center, or grocery store.

If your goal is to be an upscale luxury spa or exclusive esthetics business, you might consider locations with a golf course or country club nearby. Whatever you choose, be sure to do a drive-by or walk-by at various times of day to assess the potential success of the location(s) you are considering.

USING YOUR SPACE

Another thing to ponder as you assess your location options is what you intend to do with your space. As mentioned earlier, not everybody needs to be a day spa. In fact, some day spas are struggling because they haven't kept up with *the lives of women*. In this chapter, we will discuss in simplified terms the "profit per square foot" formula that you can use to determine which aspects of your business are most profitable.

Facial department: Calculate how much square footage your facial department contains and divide that number into the total income that department generates in a month (or year or whatever). The resulting number is generally your "profit per square foot, per month."

Then you can do the same with all other departments in your spa for comparison. (You can get more technical by figuring in your costs of running each department, but for purposes of simplicity, we are not doing that here.)

Odds are that the income generated by your manicure and pedicure spaces or your massage room does not compare to what comes from your facial room, simply because of the unique retail opportunities afforded by esthetic services. *And if that is not the case, then likely your facial department's retail sales are below where they should be.*

So for increased profit, you might want to consider eliminating nails and/or massage and adding an additional facial room, which very well could be a better use of space for you.

I understand that many spa owners believe that if clients want a service, then it should be offered. And during the early days of the day spa, that made sense. However, if increased income is your goal in this business, then you may need to re-think your priorities.

While it is a nice gesture to offer non-profitable services, unless your other *more profitable* services are providing the extra income to cover what is being lost (or you don't mind forfeiting that lost income), it may not be a wise choice for you.

Make the *"most profit per square foot"* ratio a goal in your business. If you are devoting a lot of square footage to something that is not bringing you the income that you desire, get rid of it and instead use that space to expand another of your more profitable departments.

Here are some examples of low- or non-revenue producing space:

- Large waiting area
- Relaxation area
- Lockers/changing area
- Nail stations/massage[12]
- Large break area for staff

---

[12] *Eliminating these services is typically not an option for Resort Spas.*

7. EFFECTIVE MARKETING

Marketing your business without first defining your brand or image and determining your target market rarely works, and in fact is a big mistake and a monumental waste of money. So before embarking on a marketing campaign, you must determine *who you want to be*.

How do you want to be identified: Trendy, anti-aging, clinical, tranquil, cosmopolitan, exclusive, girly, masculine, unisex? Once that has been decided, your marketing strategies should always further your brand.

Selling Treatments....or Creating Loyal Clients?
Our "bread and butter" in this business comes from our loyal and long-term clients. They are the ones whose income we can count on throughout the life of our business. So give it some careful thought when choosing your marketing tactics.

Offering discounted services may bring new bodies in your door, but once the discounted price is gone, so will be the client. Instead, choose marketing strategies that will serve the goal of creating long-term, loyal clients; clients that will make and keep regular appointments and will purchase retail products from you. Treat them well, for at any moment, we are only one mistake away from losing them to another spa.

DEFINING YOUR TARGET MARKET

Before choosing a marketing strategy, you must research and carefully consider your demographic.[13] Determine where your desired clientele gets their information and don't be afraid to think outside the box a little.

If you own a young, trendy waxing studio, social media is great, but don't overlook college publications and local gyms. If your business is in upscale suburbia, think about golf and country clubs, yoga and Pilates studios, and places where mommies might hang out such as gymnastics and karate studios.

KNOW YOUR CUSTOMERS

Before planning a service menu or selecting a product line, you must consider whether your clients will be predominantly women, men, college students, Baby Boomers, etc.

Baby Boomers are those currently in their 50s and 60s. They are often our best clients because they are most interested in anti-aging products and services, and they typically have the disposable income to afford it.

In many cases, however, this demographic may not be actively involved with social media, and there's a pretty good chance that

---

[13] *Demographic: A statistic characterizing human populations (or segments of human populations broken down by age or sex or income, etc.).*

some of them may not prefer online scheduling. So if you are utilizing strictly social media and online services to connect, you could be missing out on an extremely profitable group of potential clients.

You should also contemplate the income level, ethnicity(s), and possible time constraints when setting your menu. Income level obviously relates to pricing, ethnicity dictates what types of treatments will do well on your menu, and it is imperative to consider the needs of working women and stay-at-home moms regarding your menu, and hours and days of operation.

Once you have determined your demographic, you can then more capably decide whether to offer spa treatments, clinical treatments, or both, as well as what level of products to use and sell.

Here are some points to consider when contemplating your desired demographic:

BABY BOOMER:
("Baby Boomer" – those born during a demographic birth boom of 1946-1964, following World War II.)

- Those born in 1950+ are typically very interested in proper skin care.

- They may have more money to spend.

- They may be well-educated.

- They may have special needs regarding diminishing eyesight which can affect reading of your marketing materials and packaging. This can be resolved with a larger font and contrasting colors on your marketing literature, and brighter lighting in your retail area.

▶ This is your opportunity to specialize in the lucrative anti-aging market.

WOMEN: *Generally enjoy the shopping experience.*

Do NOT like:

- To bend down to grab a product *(exception: younger women).*

- The Butt Brush Factor.[14]

- To buy on their way out *(encourage shopping* **before** *treatment).*

Do LIKE:

- To read the front of the package before buying *(this is* ***crucial****).*

- To spend more time and money when shopping with a friend.

- Mirrors = self-interest, primping *(but it slows down the exit process, so beware of mirrors inside your treatment room).*

---

[14] *When product displays are placed in a location that causes passersby to brush up against the shopper.*

MEN: *Generally do <u>not</u> enjoy the shopping experience.*

- Shop like they drive *(fast; so be ready!)*.

- Be sure to have packages at the front desk, ready to go.

- Be sure to keep records of their wives' and significant others' retail items and purchases.

- They like having signs and written info available.

- It's a good idea to have some male-oriented displays, names of products, posters, testers.

KIDS:

- Huge underdeveloped opportunity for specialized products.

- Offer college dorm skin care kits.

- Have simple and quick facial treatments on your menu.

- Have acne treatments on your menu.

- Offer skin care education on-site (either your site or theirs).

SENIORS:

- Advertise in church newsletter, senior care facilities.

- Opportunity for specialized treatments and home care products for very mature skin.

- Offer easy home care product replenishment options.

- Senior discounts are appreciated.

- Include transportation options in your marketing efforts.

Measurable Marketing

There is a very important aspect in marketing efforts that is too often overlooked. When you spend your hard-earned money on any sort of marketing strategy, you should have some way to measure its success. This means you should be able to track responses such as phone calls or visits to the spa, any purchases, or new client appointments, etc.

If you can't measure it, it's not worth your money. You must entice the reader (or listener) to take action. Otherwise, how will you know it worked?

Ban the Clutter

An effective marketer knows that in order for his or her product and message to stand out, it needs to be very clear and to the point -- and all the *blah-blah-blah* a prospective customer doesn't need to hear must be omitted. This means you must leave out anything that will make your message get lost among everything else competing for the customer's attention.

Any marketing message – *if it's going to get results* – needs to cut through the clutter. If the message is unclear, too complex, or too long, it won't *cut through*, and the marketer has failed to engage the customer. In essence, the message falls on deaf ears.

MARKETING IDEAS

If you build it, will they come?

Of course, I highly recommend seeking out the advice of qualified advisors. Even the most successful business people don't necessarily have all the answers all of the time, but they are wise enough to seek out qualified expertise in those areas where they need assistance. And by "qualified," I mean you must carefully evaluate the people who have your ear.

For example, the advice to new estheticians is typically the same on the subject of how to build a client base: *"Hand out your business card!" "Collect email addresses!" "Send emails!"* That is great advice for any business that relies on transient customers. But is that the best method of marketing for businesses such as ours which are built on relationships? *(No!)*

Let's explore other marketing options that are more specific to the esthetics business:

K.I.S.S. (Keep It Simple, Sweetheart)
The least expensive and most direct way of reaching clients is so simple: Invite them in! Grab a friend, hand him or her a pen and paper and drive around the neighborhoods where you would like to snag yourself some new clients. (Obviously, the nearer to your business, the better.)

As you drive down the various streets, have your co-pilot simply write down addresses. Then prepare a nice "Dear Neighbor" letter to send to those prospective new clients. Add your contact info, hours of operation, product lines used, your menu, business card, etc.

I suggest printing this on specialty paper that you can buy at your local office supply store. And if you get decorative envelopes, it will help it stand out and hopefully save it from death by recycle bin. I urge you to hand-address the envelopes so it appears more personal, *which is exactly what you are going for.*

If you were to compare the price of the paper and postage to the cost of professionally printing a flyer or postcard, or placing an ad in a newspaper, you will find that this method of marketing is much less expensive *and much more personal.*

Here is an outline of this very simple letter that you can personalize to fit your own business:

Dear Neighbor,

My name is Ethel Esthetician and I am the *(owner of / esthetician at)* Spa Perfection, which has just opened in the Happy Valley Shopping Center.

I am writing to introduce myself and to invite you to come in for a complimentary _____ *(skin evaluation, brow wax, product sample).*

I have been in the business for _____ years, my specialty is _____ *(and then add something personal about yourself. What makes you special? What do you do better than anyone else in your area? Give them a list. For example:)*

- No double dipping with wax services
- Stellar sanitation practices
- Post-grad education
- Organic products
- Ample parking

- Safe location
- Evening hours
- Your specialty
- High-tech equipment
- Aromatherapy specialist
- No animal testing
- Massage therapist
- Nail technician
- Body treatments
- Extra-wide facial bed for larger clients
- Less disrobing in body treatments
- Abbreviated facial treatments
- Customized facials
- VIP program

I am enclosing a copy of my menu for you. I hope that you will stop in for your complimentary service. I look forward to meeting you.

Thank you for taking the time to read my letter. I hope to see you soon.

Sincerely,

Ethel Esthetician

Assess the Competition
And while you are out there driving around, also check out all spas and estheticians in your neighborhood, or even within a couple of miles. If you can grab a brochure, do it. If not, at least write down the name of the business and see if you can get some info online.

Figure out if there is a void, some service that none of them are offering (or at least not actively promoting). And perhaps you will find your specialty! It may require that you take a few extra esthetic classes, but so what? Become really good at whatever it is the others are *not* doing, and get the word out that you specialize in this service.

Here are some specialty ideas:

- Organic treatments
- Peels
- Clinical anti-aging
- Clinical acne treatments
- Teens and 'Tweens facial treatments
- Treatments for mature skin (60+)
- De-stress/Aromatherapy treatments
- Lunchtime "Quickie Facial" or "Happy Hour Facial"
- Stand-alone eye treatments
- Peel treatment for hyperpigmented hands or décolleté
- Facial treatment specifically for pregnant women
- Warm winter treatments (heated blanket, winter scents and decorations. *"Winter Wonderland" theme)*
- Cool summer treatments (cool towels, no steam. Omit heated hand treatments. *"Lei Spa" theme)*
- Imagery/subliminal facial with earphones (weight loss, de-stress, etc.)

Newsletters

As discussed earlier, it is important to make consistent efforts to provide great customer service. The newsletter is an under-used and under-valued method of reaching out to clients and keeping your name in front of them so you are not forgotten. It is a great way to impart education, information and to promote your products and services.

This is not to be confused with e-newsletters and emails. For all the reasons set forth in Chapter 4, the impact of e-newsletters has faded. That's not to say it won't come back as a driving force someday, but as of this writing it is not the best way to reach out to the majority of esthetics clients.

Newsletters do not have to be professionally prepared. They can be created on your computer using typical word processing software. It can be as simple as one page, and it can be sent monthly or quarterly -- as long as it is sent regularly.

Be sure to provide some sort of educational tidbit in your newsletter such as proper sunscreen use, makeup tips, skin cancer statistics -- all of which can be gleaned from a quick internet search of public information sites. Or provide an easy-to-understand explanation of esthetic terms such as *exfoliation, antioxidant* and *peptides*.

And always be certain to mention a service or product that you offer that relates to the topic in your newsletter. In other words, present a skin care problem or dilemma, *and then offer the solution!*

Hair Salon & Spa

Are there opportunities to have one-on-one time with clients while they are in the stylist's chair? Will the owner of the salon allow you to give hand massages while the client is under the dryer or foil?

Would you be allowed to offer the hair stylists a free treatment in exchange for any clients that they refer to you? Would those hair stylists be interested in participating in your marketing plan (and if so, will they represent you well?) Lots of questions, I know -- with no hard-and-fast answers. This is where your creativity and personality comes in.

Mystery Gift Card

This is a fun way to entice people to come into your business. Be sure to indicate a specific timeframe for this promotion so it does not go on indefinitely. It should feel exciting and special to the clients.

Send an email that says:

"This email is worth up to $200!
Print out this email and stop by the spa on Saturday or Sunday, November 3rd or 4th to exchange your email print-out for a surprise gift card worth $20 to $200 in services or 10% to 20% off of retail products!"

Have a basket that they can reach into and randomly pull out a card that tells them what their discount will be. It's a really fun way to get people in, surprise them and reward them. And because specific action on their part is required, it is *measureable*, and therefore easy to determine if this is a successful marketing strategy for you.

Partner with a Charity

Very often, charities hold organized events such as where groups of people form teams and participate in local activities. Not only is it a great way to support a wonderful charity, but it exposes your business to large groups of women in your area.

Wish List

Create a "Wish List" for each of your female clients which includes her favorite esthetic or spa treatments and her favorite products. Be sure to update the Wish List regularly throughout the year, as this list can be used for Valentine's Day, Mother's Day, birthday, Christmas, etc.

After getting permission from the women to contact their spouse or significant other, contact their partner to let them know that you have their love's Wish List. Men in particular will be thrilled that they no longer must struggle with getting the right gift, yet the specifics of the gift will still be a surprise to her.

Say it with Flowers

A $25 bouquet of flowers sent to your best female clients for their birthdays, or maybe after three client referrals, is an inexpensive yet powerful marketing tool. It is so much more impactful than the 10% discount that is typically offered.

Not only is a gift of flowers unexpected, but what woman doesn't love receiving flowers? You will have made a huge impression on her. And if you send it to her workplace, think of the impact this lovely gesture will have on other women who see it! They will all want to know where the flowers came from. *(Her esthetician!)* And, voila, new clients!

The Younger Generations

Consider offering a presentation for middle-schoolers and high-schoolers (and their moms!) on the subject of proper skin care. Definitely take a Skin Scanner[15] or some sort of evaluation tool with you as it will generate a lot of interest and hold everybody's attention. I've done this many times and let me warn you, allow more time than you think you'll need. People are fascinated with the Skin Scanner!

With permission, you can do this after school or at lunchtime on the school grounds, or invite a Boy Scout or Girl Scout troop, sports team or class to your place of business. Another idea is to

---

[15] *Previously discussed in Chapter 3, Client Development Plan.*

donate a group consultation to a school auction in your area.

Another neglected group of potential retail customers are college students. Skin care kits should be on every college student's shopping list, but it rarely is. So create a College Student Skin Care Kit and keep it really simple because college dorms do not have a lot of space. And especially with boys, not too many products.

Be sure they have a super simple way to reorder their Skin Care Kit (by text or email preferably) by arranging to have mom's credit card info and the student's college shipping address noted in your file.

Ladies' Holiday Party

Choose an evening or weekend afternoon – whatever will work best for the majority of your clients – and throw a get-together at your spa or studio. If your location is small, make it an Open House so that your guests' arrival times will vary.

With women, you've got to plan a little more ahead than for men. 30 days ahead is not too far in advance to throw this girls' holiday shindig. Just be sure you have thought this through well in advance and have ordered your Christmas and holiday retail plenty early.

Make some easy appetizers (in my experience, women don't usually eat much, so don't go overboard), serve hot tea or wine or whatever works for you. Get the fun holiday music going; choose the livelier music as it will set a happy tone for your party and encourage people to buy. Offer whatever easy services you can, such as chair massage, hand massage, heated hand mitt treatments, eye mask treatments, etc.

This is a great time to have a "sale" table with discounted products that you want to get rid of, as long as they still have a suitable shelf life, of course. Have your holiday gift items wrapped and displayed very prominently in the room so your clients can follow their impulsive shopping instincts!

And always keep stocking stuffers in mind; little things that clients will buy as hostess gifts for holiday parties they may be going to, or to give to teachers, or for holiday gift exchanges, and other holiday events.

One very important tip: Be certain to bring somebody in to help you with this event. You will be wearing many hats that day: Salesperson, cashier, marketing executive, concierge, esthetician and janitor. It's a good idea to have somebody there to help, or by the end of the event you will feel that you did not get to pay enough attention to many of your guests.

Remember, your guests won't necessarily know each other because usually they are coming in individually for their appointments, so it's best for you to be the hostess while somebody else helps out with ringing up sales, wrapping gifts, pouring wine, whatever. Even if you have to pay somebody a couple of hours' wages, it will be worth it.

Men's Holiday Evening

Historically, men are last-minute Christmas and holiday shoppers. And while they probably know that the women in their lives love facials and massage and other spa services, they don't always completely understand the ritual and/or the purpose. So we've got to make it really easy for them to give us their business, which means they must feel comfortable walking into our spa or skin care business.

I suggest picking one night, preferably a week or two before Christmas, and hold a Men's Shopping Night (No Ladies Allowed). You want to hold this event obviously before Christmas – before the men have already done their Christmas shopping, but not so far in advance that men's brains aren't yet in holiday mode.

Advertise the event by way of newspaper ad or mailers if you want to invite the general public, or send holiday-themed postcards[16] to clients' homes if you prefer to keep it exclusive.

You can make this a big event by offering food and drink and free chair massages, if you have that option. Or you can simply offer a hot drink and a shopping bag for the men to fill. Men typically do not enjoy the shopping experience as much as women do, so plan accordingly.

Always try to make things easy for the men who may have never previously stepped into a spa or esthetics business. If you are hoping to gain some male facial clients, then do what you can to get rid of the girly decorations for the evening so it feels a bit more gentlemen-friendly.

Put up signs advertising your Gentlemen's services (if you don't already have men's services on your menu, create some!). Place your men's products up front and center and have testers available so men can feel and smell the products while they are there.

If you've got a brother, boyfriend or husband, bring him in to assist you that night, even if it is just as a greeter. Men will feel more comfortable if they are not the only man in the room. They

---

[16] *There are inexpensive postcards that you can order from the many online print marketing companies.*

will be likely to linger longer which will translate into more purchases and a better rapport.

Have holiday gifts packaged and ready-to-go. Most men want to get in, make their purchase, and get out. So have gift certificates ready to go and be sure they are contained in something attractive. If he has to wrap it himself, he may not come back next year.

Even if it's just a holiday envelope from your local office supply store, make it special. Make an impact whenever you can because word-of-mouth is your best advertisement. And be sure you make a note of what he bought so that you can refer to it next year!

It is vital that your holiday items are gift-wrapped or that you can wrap them quickly. Even if you don't usually offer gift wrapping, this is the season to change the rules. At the very least, buy some bags at your local wholesale florist/gift store along with some holiday tissue.

Do whatever you have to do so that your gifts are grab-and-go. This is not just true for men, this is the way to attract all impulse holiday shoppers.

Men are very loyal customers, and once your Men's Holiday Evening becomes well-known, it will be an annual event that more and more men (and their significant others) will depend on and look forward to every year!

Other Party Themes

You can throw a shindig any time of year with varying themes. How about a Summer Tropical party? Play Hawaiian music, serve tropical drinks, highlight your sunscreen and other summer products and, of course, your Tantalizing Tropical Treatments.

This is a great way to showcase your sandal-worthy foot treatments, if you have any.

The same thing can be done during winter, instead highlighting your Warm Winter Treatments and hydrating products.

8. FORMULA FOR PROSPERITY

There are no two ways about it: **Retail is king in the spa world**. It is maximum profit with minimum effort.

It's very easy to assess profitability when you compare facial services to retail: Facial treatments require time and overhead, such as an esthetician who must be compensated, cost of back bar product, laundry, furniture, etc.

On the other hand, retail sales require nothing but a little shelf space. And once a customer is hooked on the importance of home care products as a result of her facial, she will replenish her supply repeatedly on her own. A $200 purchase of skin care products can happen in 10 minutes or less in the spa or online, and it is pure profit for the spa.

So basically all roads to the financial success of an esthetics business lead to retail. And successful retailing of skin care products begins long before the customer ever walks through the door of the business.

There is a specific science behind why people buy. And for those of us in esthetics, there is a simple but very important formula that we must follow. It contains 5 vital elements, as follows:

1. Product Line
2. Menu
3. Intake Process
4. Esthetician
5. Home Care Products

1. Product Line

The first step is the perfect product line. And by "perfect," I mean: Fits the business's goals, has low (or preferably *no*) minimum order requirements, offers product knowledge education for estheticians, offers samples of products, has lots of really great serums, easy-to-use masks, and packaging that fits your image. And most importantly, it produces the visible results that your clientele is looking for.

❧ NOTE to SPA OWNERS:

*It is vital that you involve your estheticians in the research and selection of skin care products. Skin care product lines are not created equal, and **if an esthetician doesn't love the products she is required to use, the spa's profit will suffer**. I once consulted with a spa whose Spa Director was a massage therapist with a background in hotel management. Maybe this sounds good on paper, but in actuality, the spa was suffering. She had no training or understanding about esthetics equipment, products, ingredients or facial services. (This is not something that you can learn by simply working in a spa environment.) This is relatively common, as owners of spas often incorrectly assume that someone who has worked in any capacity in a spa is therefore qualified to manage the esthetics department. It is simply not true,* and you are hurting your business. You <u>must</u> incorporate a trained and qualified esthetician into important decision-making. That's the only way to protect your bottom line.

2. Menu

The service menu needs to read a specific way in order to entice guests to have a treatment. Potential clients are not interested in the ingredient deck of the products used in the facial. They don't necessarily know what "collagen" is, or why it matters. They don't know what Vitamin C does for the skin. They likely don't recognize the brand name of your products when they are first introduced to them.

As previously discussed in Chapter 5, potential clients have only one question in their minds when assessing a menu, and that is, *"What's in it for me?"* In other words, *"How will this facial benefit me?"* But few will ask this question out loud. Instead they will put the menu down and never look back.

Examples of simple and effective facial descriptions for any skin type:

- **European Facial -** *This perfect facial will be customized to deep-clean and balance any skin type using highly-effective serums with active ingredients from plants, berries and fruits:*

- **Dry skin** *will be nourished, hydrated, rejuvenated and moisturized.*

- **Sensitive skin** *will be soothed, even-toned and gently hydrated.*

- **Combination skin** *will be balanced, purified and hydrated.*

- **Oily skin** *will be purified and balanced.*

- **Problematic skin** *will be deep-cleaned, purified, soothed and decongested.*

Like every other new, excited and inexperienced spa owner, I spent hours agonizing over how to create the *perfect* menu. But I learned over the years that the service menu is not a place that I need to spend a lot of money because the truth of the matter is that these days, paper menus do not make or break a spa.

People look at services online more often than they look at hard copy spa menus, which are barely glanced at before being thrown away. For that reason, I suggest you create your own menus using basic computer software.

The beauty of the DIY menu is that you can edit, rearrange, delete, change prices, colors, and themes seasonally, or any time you want to. You can even create your own promotional flyer to stick inside your menu any time the mood strikes you. It keeps things fresh and interesting, which is a great thing for your business.

Creating the menu on your computer will also save you time and extra postage because you can tri-fold it and mail it in a regular letter-sized envelope.

There are lots of places where you should not scrimp or cut corners, but your menu isn't one of them.

3. The Intake Process
The intake process is extremely important for reasons of client

safety, of course, but it is also the place where the retail sales begin as the esthetician discusses the client's skin care goals and current home care regimen.

A huge mistake that most spas make is skipping this vital step with first-time clients. This is where a bond and trust is created between the esthetician and the client that leads to repeat customers and continued retail sales long after they have exited the esthetic business or spa.

I believe that estheticians are better off creating their own intake form so that it is specific to their particular esthetic practice. I am not suggesting a professionally-made Intake Form. As with the Menu of Services, I prefer to create it on my own computer so I can print and edit, as needed.

Here are some suggestions that you can pick from to use in your intake form as they apply to you *(I am not suggesting that you need <u>all</u> of these)*:

1. SKIN SCANNER EVALUATION

    - Sun damage: Mild, moderate or severe; *and location.*

    - Dehydration: Mild, moderate or severe; *and water consumption*

    - Skin type, Fitzpatrick type, Glogau scale

2. MANUAL EVALUATION

    - Deep wrinkles; *location*

    - Closed comedones; *location*

- Open comedones; *location*
- Enlarged pores; *location*
- Capillaries; *location*
- Acne; *location and grade*
- Suspicious moles; *location*

3. MEDICAL HISTORY

    - Previous referral to dermatologist; *reason*
    - Allergies
    - Medications that may be affecting the client's skin
    - Pregnant or nursing
    - Current health conditions that may be affecting the client's skin
    - Recent or pending cosmetic surgeries, or injectibles; *when?*
    - Retin A or Accutane use; *when?*
    - Sunbathed or tanning bed within 14 days?
    - Smoker?

4. CONTRAINDICATIONS (if using electrical esthetic equipment)

   - Metal implants
   - Pacemaker
   - Epileptic
   - Pregnant

5. ISSUES and GOALS

   - Top 3 skin care complaints (or goals)
   - Previous skin care treatments? *How often?*
   - Likes and dislikes about previous facials, *if any?*

6. HOME CARE

   - Over-the-counter, Department Store, Professional or MLM[17]
   - Frequency of cleansing per day
   - Tools used; *hands, loofah, washcloth, sponge, cotton pads*
   - Toner
   - Moisturizer
   - Exfoliant

---

[17] *Multi-Level-Marketing.*

- Serums

- Eye Cream

- Sun Block

- Other

7. NOTES and RECORDS

- This is SO important! The last page should have a column on the left for "date" and 2 or 3 blank lines directly across the page so you can jot down the specifics of the treatment you gave that day, the products and equipment used, and any personal notes about the client's recent activities that may have had an effect on her skin.

  This reference will help you to vary the products you use at her next appointment so the treatment is not exactly the same, and to inquire about the results of the previous facial and any other pertinent personal info that you noted.

4. Esthetician

Estheticians, of course, are the hub of any esthetic department. Therefore, they must be properly trained, including Product Knowledge classes from any and all product lines they are using. Estheticians who work in a spa environment with transient clientele must be really good with people, *especially with women*.

Esthetician employees should be given incentives such as

commission paid on retail sales, and vouchers[18] or discounts on products to encourage them to use the products on themselves at home so that they are intimately familiar with each and every product. That, above all else, will lead to easy retail sales for them and profit for their employer.

5. Home Care Retail

I'm pretty sure that few (if any) estheticians working today got into this business with the goal to be a salesperson. Yet the sale of home care products is a fundamental part of an esthetician's job, for many reasons.

If an esthetician is properly trained, retail sales will happen organically, with no "hard sell" tactics needed. So it is up to the esthetician to figure out what retail sales approach best fits him or her. For me, the foundation for the client's purchase of home care retail products happens during the facial. It might begin during the Intake Process as I discuss the products the client is currently using at home, and it will most assuredly continue as I explain to the new client the products I have chosen to use during the facial.

By the time the facial is over, without fail, the client is asking me for my recommendations for home care products. With very little effort, a retail sale is made and a loyal client is born.

It is the esthetician's *duty* to provide home care education and recommendations for their clients, including written "how-to" instructions. It's our job to educate clients about the benefits of the retail products and explain clearly that proper home care

---

[18] *I prefer giving vouchers for a certain retail dollar amount which the employee can spend herself or give to a friend or family member. This will eliminate the common problem of employees purchasing unlimited products at a discount for others.*

extends the benefits of the facial treatment, which will result in continued good skin health.

It is the also the esthetician's job to make sure clients are comfortable with the ingredients and sufficiently understand the benefits of each product. In order to assure repeat retail sales, it is vital that clients feel confident that the products will be a worthwhile investment for them. And for that to happen, the esthetician *must believe it*!

Retail profits will surely suffer if the esthetician doesn't believe in the products she is selling, and that's another reason that manufacturers' Product Knowledge classes are essential. Even if the esthetician manages to sell the products once, odds are pretty high that the client won't buy them a second time.

It is also the esthetician's responsibility to keep records of client purchases for future reference. That way, the client can easily replenish his or her home care products with or without assistance from the esthetician. I regularly get requests from long-term clients asking for things like "the stuff in the silver bottle" or "my morning face wash" or "my spritzer." I know that means "serum," "cleanser" and "toner," but I have to rely on the client's file to see which specific product she is currently using.

YOUR RETAIL AREA

Retail Rocks!

The Decompression Zone
This area is comprised of the first 10 feet as a client enters your place of business. Clients' habits have been studied and analyzed, and there are a few helpful things you should know.

Initiating Contact
Give the client a chance to breathe before presenting her with questions about why she has come in. A friendly "hello" will suffice until she has had a chance to survey the area and hone in on whatever it is she may be interested in. Once she has done that, then inquire how you might help her.

It's also important *not* to ask "yes" or "no" questions such as "May I help you?" ("NO") It is better to ask, "How can I help you?"

Signage
Often I am asked whether prices should be made available on or near the retail products. My answer is a resounding YES! Definitely provide pricing so as to avoid sticker shock. It is embarrassing for a shopper to have to ask the price of something and then realize he or she can't afford it. We must avoid causing any discomfort to someone who has come into our business hoping to spend their money with us.

As touched upon earlier, we also must keep in mind that by age 40 our anti-aging clients' eyesight has begun to diminish somewhat. So be sure that any written information is at least a .12

font, if you can.

Research has shown that 91% of consumers will read the information on the front of a product's packaging and 43% will also read the back. And we all know how small that printing can be at times.

Think about placing a pretty magnifying glass on the shelf within easy reach to assist the shopper as he or she attempts to read the small print. And be sure to keep it very clean. *(That's an example of going the extra mile to provide fabulous customer service!)*

Display

Research shows that the best-selling location on the retail shelves is at bulls-eye level. The next best selling location is just slightly right of that.

It is important to move your products around regularly, in sync with your regularly-scheduled appointments. So if most of your clients come in every 4 to 6 weeks for a treatment, that's when you should modify your retail area somewhat, either by rearranging the products on the shelf or by changing the decorations. Just a little minor tweaking will do.

Also determined from research into what compels people to buy is that shoppers are hesitant to disturb an "artsy" display. Meaning if a product they want to purchase is part of a dramatic display, they won't touch it.

The same thing goes for the last product on the shelf. Shoppers don't like to take the last of anything, so always try to have more than one package of a particular product on the shelf. If you don't want to have a large back stock of products, just order some of that product's empty packaging for your display. Your shelves will look full, and no one will be the wiser.

And lastly, big department stores put a lot of money into studying what sorts of displays will lure shoppers, so by all means follow their lead. Do your own research by visiting the higher-end department stores and use their ideas. They have done the homework for you. All you have to do is snap some photos with your phone!

Samples

More than ever, shoppers want to touch and smell products. The good news about that is that once a client has interacted with a product, there becomes an element of ownership with that product. So if you provide shoppers with that opportunity, your retail sales will rise.

The most common and easiest way to encourage a shopper's interaction with products is by sampling, such as:

- ▶ Sample bar – This is like a toy box for adults. They are able to interact with many products at once, to try them on, to compare and to bond with them.

- ▶ Companies are not offering free samples to estheticians as often as they used to, but even if you have to purchase samples, it is a good investment in future retail sales for all of the reasons given above.

- ▶ Sampling dramatically reduces and/or completely eliminates return of products. This reason alone is worth the minimal extra expense of providing samples.

THE SHOPPING EXPERIENCE

Make it Easy
Sounds elementary, I know. But unfortunately rarely do businesses take this into consideration and plan ahead. Yet this is essential.

M.Y.O.B.
Don't ever assume how much money a client can or can't afford to spend. It is none of your business!

Credit Cards
It is unwise to dictate how clients will spend their money at your business. These days, everybody is paying by credit card so you must accept them all.

I am baffled by those who refuse to accept American Express due to the minimal extra transaction charge. Why would you not want American Express card holders to buy from you? American Express offers some great perks for cardholders, so of course they would prefer to use that card. So why force them to use a different card?

American Express also requires that the credit card balance is paid off every month, so it's a pretty safe assumption that this client is financially solvent. So I'd say do everything you can to cultivate a relationship with this client!

Girl Friends
It is a studied and proven fact that women will spend more money when they are shopping with their BFFs. That is really good news for us because we can easily use that factoid to our benefit by holding regular events for women at our places of

business.

Hands Free
Clients will only purchase as much as they can hold. So when their hands are full, they will stop shopping. When you consider that women will likely have a purse in one hand, it means they will be limited to the other hand for shopping. The solution for this is either to keep an eye out for a shopper's hands becoming full and offer to hold her products at the front desk, or have shopping bags or baskets available for her.

More is More
The more time a shopper spends in your retail area, the more money he or she will spend. So make it a pleasant experience with lots of products to sample, literature to read, and assistance with packages.

No-Fault Return Policy
Unless you have a problem client who makes a habit of using and returning products, just go ahead and take back a returned product. If it's one of your regular clients, take it back with a big smile and no questions asked. That goodwill gesture is worth a lot more in client loyalty and future purchases than you may have lost with the occasional returned product which may be outside your posted return policy date.

Online Shopping
I want to make this *very, very, very* clear: I am in **no way** supportive of estheticians and spas selling professional esthetics products online to the public. However, if an esthetician is selling products from her own website <u>via a password-protected page to her clients only *(not to the public)*,</u> that is a different matter.

In keeping with the "make it easy" theme, this is a simple way for existing clients -- who have already been through the esthetician's consultation and intake process, and have been provided a detailed home care protocol by their esthetician – to easily replenish their home care products.

Free Shipping

To make it easy and painless for clients to spend their money with you, you might consider eliminating shipping charges when sending products to existing clients. Simply raise your retail prices by a quarter or so on most (or all) of your products and, *voila!* -- that extra income will cover occasional shipping fees.

No Tipping

This is a hot button for many in the esthetics business which is certainly understandable as tipping has been part of our livelihood since esthetics broke away from being an afterthought at a hair salon. But now esthetics has become a specialty and in some cases very clinical. And for those esthetics businesses, eliminating the tipping process might be something you should consider.

While many estheticians swear that they won't treat a 20% tipper any different from a 10% tipper, it is really a tough promise to keep. They believe that they will lose income if they stop taking tips, but that is not necessarily true. In fact, sometimes the opposite is true.

If you were to raise your facial treatments 15%, it would more than likely balance out the difference between the varying tip percentages. And it would be guaranteed income, and not subject to the whims of the tipper.

When I sold my spa and went solo, that was the time that I opted to eliminate tipping. My clients came to love the fact that they do not have to calculate the tip and wonder if they are tipping enough.

For some of us, there is also the issue that we become very close friends with our clients after so many years, and the tipping issue can be awkward for everyone. For me, the best part of eliminating tipping was that it made me different. It made me stand out from other estheticians in a positive way, and who doesn't love that?

If you want to consider changing your tipping policy and raising your prices, the best time to do that is at a point when something has changed in your business so that raising your prices makes more sense. You might consider re-vamping your menu, for example, or simply adding new treatments at slightly higher prices. Or you can raise your prices if perhaps you have recently changed locations.

At the beginning of a new year is also a great time to raise prices, especially if you haven't done it in a while. Whatever you decide, it is a good idea to send a letter to clients advising them of the change. Avoid surprises that involve money.

"Retail-Only" Shoppers

Of course, ideally we would like to have all clients come in for regular facials. But realistically, that is never going to happen. So that leaves a lot of women out there purchasing products from drug stores, department stores, TV and Multi-Level-Marketing companies. Clearly they need our help!

When you are out in the world meeting people and marketing yourself, don't neglect those women whom you might only be able to convince to come in for a yearly diagnostic facial, followed by a home care protocol recommendation that they can follow until their next annual facial. It's better to have them on your high-quality professional home care products than over-the-counter, over-priced and low-quality junk.

Everything you can touch today, at some point did not exist until somebody took an idea all the way to the end.

9. LEGAL ISSUES

Liability Insurance

It is frightening how many estheticians and business owners do not understand the importance of having your own liability insurance. Often technicians employed by spas or esthetics businesses assume that they are covered by their employer's insurance. But how many have actually read the insurance policy and are 100% clear on what exactly is covered?

For example, not all electrical equipment is covered, and there are some services that are commonly excluded. As the field of esthetics becomes more clinical and high-tech, it is a mistake to assume that everything we can purchase and use will be covered by our liability insurance.

Also, how can the employee be certain that the insurance premiums are being paid in a timely manner by their employer? If the payments are delinquent, the policy will be cancelled and that means that nobody is covered.

Individual policies are not expensive…but lawsuits are!

The reason to have your own liability insurance is not because people these days are "sue happy" because actually that is not true -- at least not where personal injury is concerned. In California, for example, a mere 1.5 percent of all lawsuits filed are for personal injury issues.

The real reason to have liability insurance is that consumers have a right to expect when they come in for an advertised service, that the technician is qualified to perform that service. In other words, consumers have a right *not to be harmed*. But things happen, mistakes are made, equipment fails, and we have to protect ourselves.

Consent Forms

I know we often joke about how some people will lie in order to get a service performed, but it is true! For example, those who tell us they are not on Retin A or Accutane, or they say have not tanned recently, just so they can have their wax service performed.

It isn't a laughing matter, however, if something goes wrong and we have no proof that the client was made aware of possible contraindications before the service was performed. We could be in big trouble.

Consent forms are simple and important. Use them.

10. NETWORKING

Sometimes we get so ensconced in our treatment rooms that we lose touch with what is going on in the world of esthetics. That is how we get stuck in a rut and become stale…and that can paralyze an otherwise promising esthetic career.

With the advent of the internet came online message boards. There you can get questions answered, learn about new ingredients and equipment and find information about upcoming trade shows and educational opportunities – all without ever leaving your treatment room. And if you are a seasoned esthetician, you know that we are only as strong as our weakest link. So mentoring an esthetician who is coming up the ranks behind you *helps us all.*

One serious warning though is when participating in online message boards, be absolutely certain that you qualify your advisors. By this I mean, question their expertise.

Hidden behind their computers, people unabashedly offer information and advice that they may not be qualified to give. *So, do ask!* Ask for their credentials and experience on the topic for which they are offering advice. Especially if your money will be involved!

And don't fall prey to the "Negative Know-it-alls" who frequent free online message boards. They have nothing invested in the outcome, so those who are struggling or failing will always be the loudest and most talkative.

Having an esthetician license is not enough to qualify somebody as an expert, so beware. It's like shopping for jeans; try the advice on and see how it fits *you*. If it doesn't fit, put it down and walk away.

There are brilliant trade magazines available that you can read in hard copy or online. The authors and educators have done the work for us, all we have to do is read and learn!

Trade shows offer so many educational opportunities for very little cost and they are held throughout the country and the world. If you find yourself stuck in a rut, one trade show will change everything for you. In all of these years, I have never walked away from a trade show not being excited about at least one thing I learned, and I am always so glad that I attended.

We are lucky to be in a career that can go on for decades. It will change and evolve and we must do the same.

Clients don't leave because of financial issues. They leave because their needs were not met.

As for the clients you already have, remember this: *You don't own these clients*. They are only temporarily parked on your doorstep and will be glad to move along when they find something better. So being "good enough" isn't *good enough*.

But a client that has successfully bonded with his or her esthetician will not leave. The esthetician-client bond must be nurtured always. It is built on trust and loyalty. Even if there are lower prices, better locations, and prettier décor out there somewhere, there is no better *you*.

*A loyal client is a gift. Treat her well.
And be grateful.*

*She who argues her limitations…
gets to keep them.*

ABOUT THE AUTHOR

After motherhood lured her away from a successful (but inflexible) career as a court reporter and business owner, Diane Buccola obtained her esthetician license in the state of California in 1999. Her ultimate goal was to be the owner of a day spa -- not necessarily an esthetician working in the treatment room indefinitely. However, the bond with her clients kept her in the treatment room for 13 years.

Diane sold her spa and opened a solo esthetics practice in 2004. this allows her more time to work as an esthetics consultant and trainer, which is her true passion. In 2006, she created SpaBizBoard.com, a popular online subscription message board and learning tool for the spa industry which she actively participates in and manages. In her continuing effort to raise the standards of esthetics, she serves as an author and speaker on subjects related to the business side of Esthetics.

Shortly after the NCEA Certified Professional Esthetician certification became available, Diane met the qualifications to become NCEA Certified in 2008. NCEA Certification is the highest standard of skin care certification currently available in the United States.[19]

Diane serves as a member of the Les Nouvelles Esthetiques & Spa Magazine Advisory Board and Director of the Skin Analysis Lounge at Be Well Expo[20] and has been an esthetician volunteer with the ACS Look Good Feel Better program since 2004.

---

[19] *www.NCEACertified.tv*
[20] *www.bewell-expo.com*

Made in the USA
Middletown, DE
23 February 2017